T0104101

ANIMAL FACTopia!

Follow the TRAIL of 400 BEASTLY FACTS

BY JULIE BEER

Illustrated by ANDY SMITH

BRITANNICA BOOKS

CONTENTS

ROAR, FLY, and SLITHER
back to FACTopia!
Get ready, because things are about to get wild.

Prepare for a fact-filled animal adventure that explores hundreds of Earth's feathery, scaly, creepy, cuddly, and dangerous creatures. For example...

Did you know ants don't have ears? They "listen" by feeling vibrations with their legs.

Get a leg up on more. Like the strawberry poison frog, which is red all over except for its bright blue legs—the source of its nickname, the "blue jeans" frog.

They're not the only things that are blue. An Arctic reindeer's eyes change from gold in the summer to deep blue during the chilly winter.

Brr! Keep cozy with survival strategies from amazing animals like the Arctic fox, which wraps its fluffy tail around its body like a blanket to stay warm.

You might have spotted that there is something special about being here in FACTopia. Every fact is *linked to the next*, and in the most surprising and even hilarious ways.

On this FACTopia adventure you will discover creatures from the **deepest seas** to the **hottest deserts** to **grand grasslands**—and even beasts that roamed Earth in **prehistoric times**. Discover what each turn of the page will bring!

But there isn't just one trail through this book. Your path branches every now and then, and you can **hop backward** or **gallop forward** → — to a totally different (*but still connected*) part of FACTopia.

Let your curiosity take you wherever it leads. Of course, a good place to start could be right here, at the beginning...........

For example, take this detour

to find out about perfect paws

Go to page 184

A newborn female African elephant weighs about as much as…

Speaking of elephants

...26 newborn human babies

An elephant can hold abo

African elephants gain the nickname "**tuskers**"
when their tusks grow so long they touch the ground

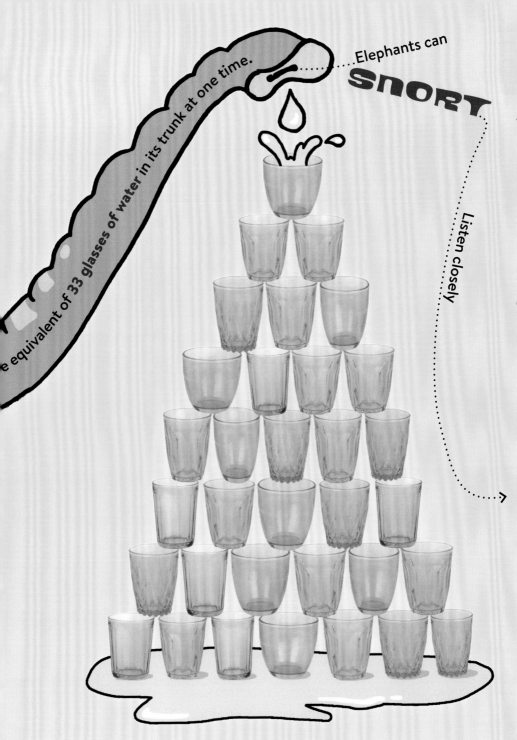

An elephant can hold the equivalent of 33 glasses of water in its trunk at one time.

Elephants can **SNORT**

Listen closely

A lanternfish's body has organs that emit light, allowing the fish to glow in the dark.

When threatened, the walnut sphinx caterpillar compresses itself like an accordion, letting out a shrill whistling sound from holes along the sides of its body.

Fireflies can glow green, yellow, and orange.

Green sea turtles get their name from the green-colored fat found under their shells.

The fossilized shell of one of the biggest turtles ever discovered is nearly 8 feet (2.4m) long and has fighting horns near its neck.

In the winter, hibernating dwarf lemurs from Madagascar survive on the fat stored in their tails.

The rattle on the end of a rattlesnake's tail is made of keratin, the same material that makes up hooves, horns, and human hair.

A type of extinct deerlike animal that lived in Florida about five million years ago had a horn on its nose shaped like a slingshot.

When opossums are under attack, they stick out their **tongues** and produce a foul **smell**, appearing to be dead.

Gentoo penguins have orange **tongues** covered in spiky bristles that help them grip and swallow fish whole.

Giving off an odor that **smells** like watermelon helps the hooded nudibranch, a species of **marine slug**, fend off predators.

Female argonaut octopuses, also called paper nautiluses, carry their **eggs** inside a special **shell** they build themselves out of a mineral secreted by their own arms.

Sea lemons are a type of **marine slug** that lay up to two million **eggs** in a structure that looks like a ribbon.

The nostrils on the **noses** of some animals like moose, hippos, and manatees close automatically when submerged **underwater**.

Tweet, tweet!

American dippers walk **underwater**! These birds are often spotted walking along the bottom of a river or stream looking for insects.

Go to page 108

One hundred million years ago, birds had teeth

Chomp down

...A group of goldfinches is called a

charm

A male white bellbird has a long piece of skin, called a wattle, that hangs from its beak. But that doesn't stop it from being the **loudest bird** on the planet. Its call is as loud as the sound coming out of a speaker at a rock concert

Five million years ago, *Pelagornis chilensis*, a seabird with a wingspan more than twice as wide as a bald eagle's, soared through the skies.

Flap your wings ······>

......The fleshy bit of skin that hangs over a male turkey's beak— meant to attract females— is called a **snood**.

The
temperature
needs to be at least
55 degrees Fahrenheit (13°C)
for a monarch butterfly's
wings to warm up—
**otherwise it
can't
fly.**

Some animals don't need wings to soar

The colugo is called a **"flying lemur,"** even though it can't actually fly and it isn't a lemur. Instead of jumping, colugos glide from tree to tree using the skin between their limbs like a wingsuit, looking for their next meal of leaves and fruit......

The largest species of flying squirrels, which glide between trees, is as **big as a house cat**...

...Flying fish use their **winglike fins and fork-shaped tails** to glide throu

Go to page 190

Ribbit, ribbit

Sugar gliders **leap through forests at night.** They bob their heads before they "take off" to help them determine distance and altitude.

More night owls ▸

Wallace's flying frogs have **extra skin between their toes** to help them glide between tree branches and oversized toe pads to help them stick when they land.

the air. Some can "fly" the length of about 15 double-decker buses

Fabulous feet

As a warning before it sprays, a skunk will **stomp its front feet.**

Little brown bats can eat up to **3,000 insects** a night.

A barn owl's ears are placed in different spots on either side of its head. Its **lopsided ears** help it better pinpoint prey at night.

Scorpions **glow blue-green** under ultraviolet light...

If you shine a flashlight on a spider at night, its **eyes glow green.**

Eye spy →

An Arctic reindeer's eyes change from **gold** in the summer to **DEEP BLUE** in the winter.

Go to page 42

Cool colors

Don't look now

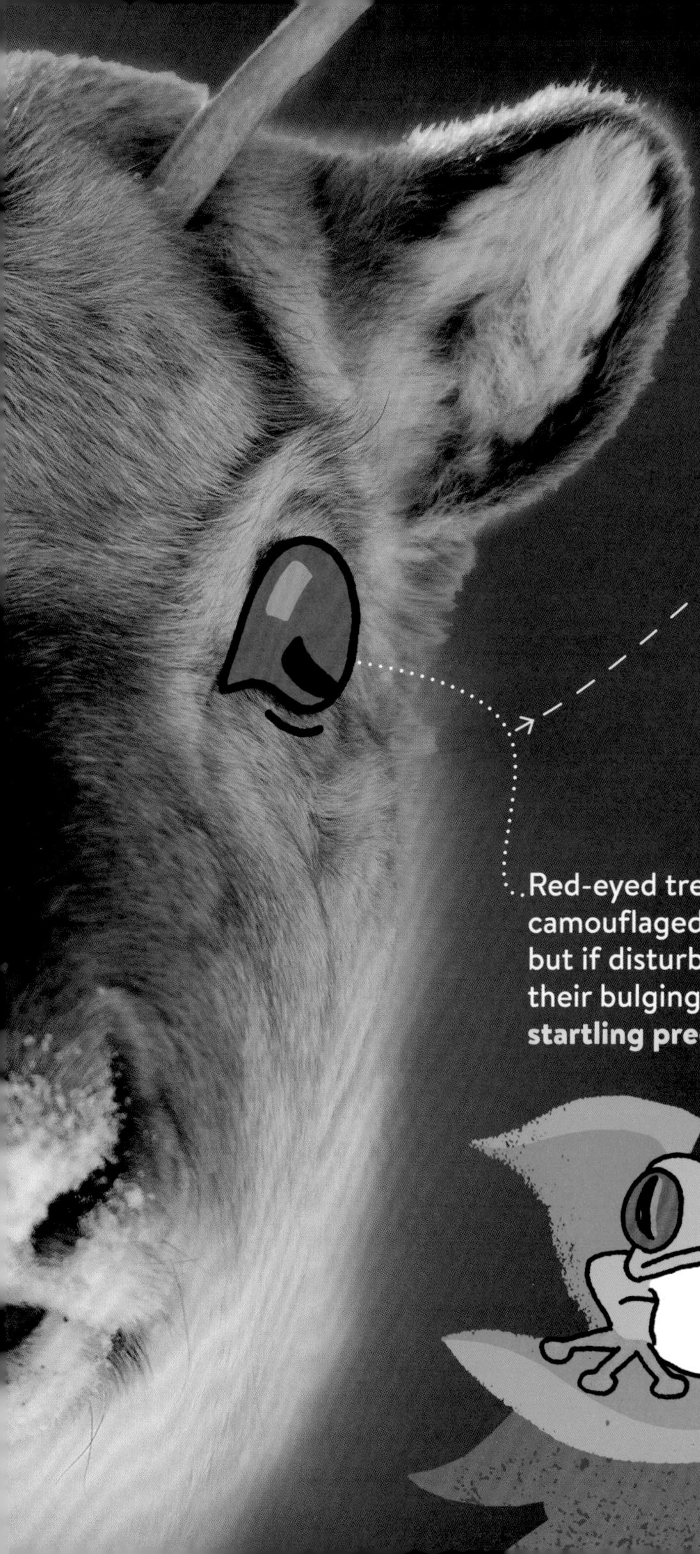

Red-eyed tree frogs sleep camouflaged on green leaves, but if disturbed they flash their bulging red eyes, **startling predators**

Snow leopards can **leap** the length of four Sumatran **rhinos** in one stride.

Great white sharks can **leap** completely out of the water while attacking prey.

Humans and **giraffes** have the same number of **bones** in their necks—seven!

Orcas are considered the top predator of the ocean—sometimes scaring away **great white sharks** from their hunting grounds.

Fossilized dinosaur **bones** can be **smelly**.

White rhinos and black **rhinos** are the same **color**—gray.

To impress females, male blue-footed boobies show off the bright **color** of their **feet** by doing a high-stepped dance.

The **back** of a **giraffe** has a small hump on it, similar to a camel's.

Some swan species swim with one of their **feet** tucked on their **backs**.

The male ring-tailed lemur, native to the African island of Madagascar, produces a **smelly** substance from its wrists, rubs it on its tail, and then waves its tail in the air to attract mates.

Island life

Go to page 106

Head to the farm

Marine iguanas of the Galápagos Islands **sneeze out extra salt** they ingest from their ocean environment, which forms a white "wig" on their head...

Looking for lizards

A **Komodo dragon** can weigh as much as a refrigerator.

The basilisk lizard can run on water for short distances to catch insects

Make a getaway

ake a quick escape from a predator

One African penguin at a German zoo escaped and accidentally wandered into the lion enclosure. Fortunately, the **lions were all asleep**, and the zookeepers led the penguin to safety using a trail of fish.

Zzzzz

Go to page 74

Hunker down

Flamingos sleep standing on one leg

A museum scientist discovered that a snail specimen, assumed to be dead after it had been collected and glued to a card, was very much alive—it had actually been **hibernating for four years**

Meerkats **.sleep in a pile**

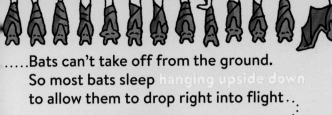

.....Bats can't take off from the ground.
So most bats sleep hanging upside down
to allow them to drop right into flight..

Whale watching

Sperm whales sleep vertically
near the surface of the ocean

Beluga whales are **born gray**—and then **turn white** once they become adults.

A blue whale's mouth can fit 100 people inside

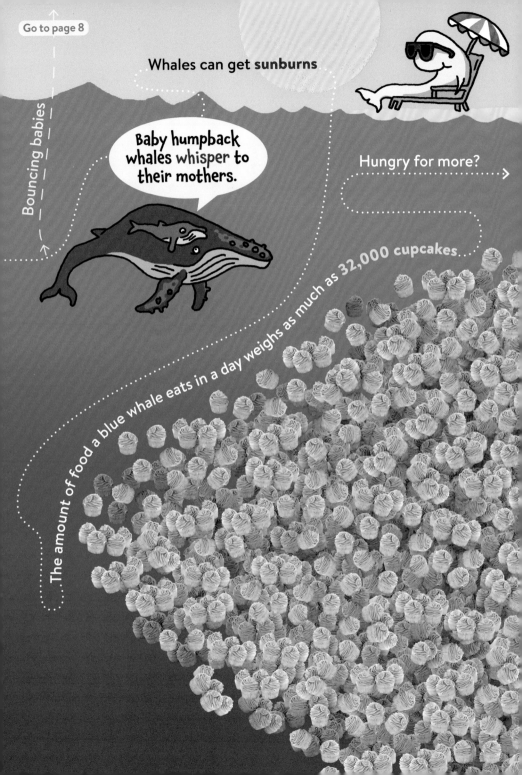

Go to page 8

Whales can get **sunburns**

Bouncing babies

Baby humpback whales whisper to their mothers.

Hungry for more?

The amount of food a blue whale eats in a day weighs as much as 32,000 cupcakes

Egg-eating snakes swallow eggs whole and then use special neck spines to break the eggshell and get at the contents inside. Then, they throw up the shell!

Platypuses don't have teeth, so they **scoop up rocks** into their cheeks to help them chew their food.

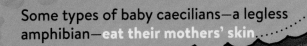

Go to page 78

Egg-cellent eggs

Super skin

Some types of baby caecilians—a legless amphibian—**eat their mothers' skin**

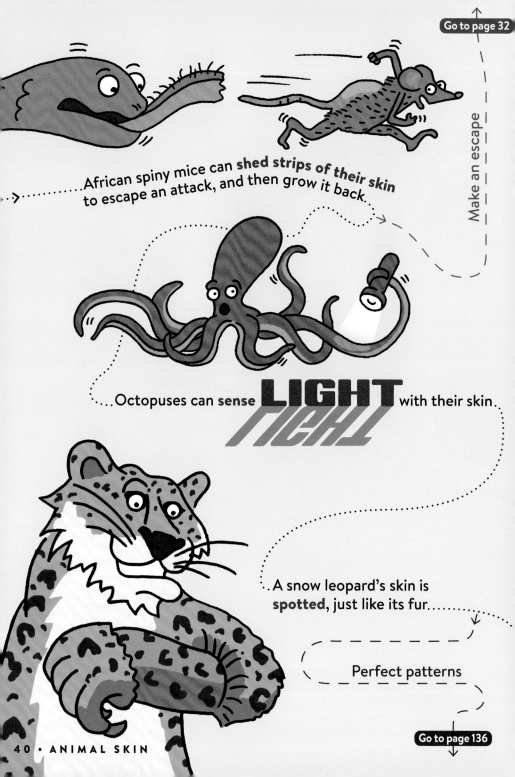

Go to page 32

Make an escape

African spiny mice can **shed strips of their skin** to escape an attack, and then grow it back.

...Octopuses can **sense** LIGHT with their skin.

A snow leopard's skin is **spotted**, just like its fur...

Perfect patterns

Go to page 136

Chameleons **change the color** of their skin to help them cool down or warm up.

So colorful

One type of salamander has no lungs. Instead, it **breathes through its skin**.

Sometimes, rare genetic mutations can cause penguins to be all **white or even yellow.**

Go to page 120

More bears

More plants

Blue-tongued skinks, a type of lizard, use their **brightly colored tongues** to scare away predators.

Pink orchid praying mantises, named for the flowering plant they resemble, trick curious insects into investigating them. Then they eat them.

Peanut worms, which live in the ocean, have **purple blood**.

Pandas have unique **black eye patches** of different shapes and sizes that scientists think may help the pandas recognize each other.

...>.....One type of pitcher plant evolved to be a **toilet for treeshrews.** When the shrew visits, it eats the plant's nectar while sitting atop the toilet bowl—shaped plant and pooping into it, providing the plant with essential nutrients......

Bee orchids are **flowers that evolved to look like female bees** in order to attract male bees that pollinate the plant.

Incredible insects

A cricket's ears are **on its legs**.

Some bumblebees can fly higher than Mount Everest

Going up!

The yellow-rumped leaf-eared mouse lives at a **higher altitude than any other mammal** in the world. It makes its home atop a 22,000-foot-high (6.7km-high) volcano!

Yaks of the Himalayas have **large lungs** that allow them to breathe in three times more air than a normal cow.

Scientists analyzed hair, poop, and bone believed to be from **abominable snowmen**. It turns out the samples were from black and brown bears that live in the Himalayas, and a dog.

Red pandas have flexible ankles that let them **climb headfirst** down trees in mountain forests in Asia.

Come on down

Some snakes in Tibet survive their cold mountain habitats by living near **hot springs**.

Blobfish don't have any muscles and look like pink oozy blobs at sea level. But in their high-pressure, deep-sea environment they look like normal swimming fish

Giant tube worms make their homes next to **deep-sea hydrothermal vents** that spew superheated water and toxic chemicals

Go to page 134

Fin-tastic fish

...The female anglerfish, which lives in the deepest parts of the ocean, uses a **spine with a glowing tip above its head** as a lure to attract prey......

Poop, sand, decay, and other bits that drift from the ocean's surface to the deep sea are called **marine snow**.

Let it snow

Because they are so hard to find, snow leopards are known as **"ghost cats."**

Canadian lynx have oversized paws that act as **snowshoes** to keep them from sinking in the snow.

Cool cats

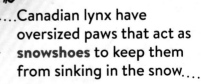

Go to page 82

Monkey around

Young snow monkeys play with snowballs.

A male proboscis monkey's

large nose

helps make its honking call louder, which warns enemies to stay away.

Go to page 114

Nice nose

After spending
time apart,
spider monkeys
greet each other
with a hug and
**wrap their tails
around one
another.**

Telling tails

To catch fis

A cheetah's tail acts like a boat's rudder to help it change directions while sprinting.

Dash on ›

guars sometimes tap the surface of water with their tails, like a lure.

Dragonflies, the **FASTEST FLYING INSECTS**, catch 95 percent of the prey they chase.

Sailfish speed through the water as fast as a car drives on the highway.

The mammal with the **fastest heartbeat** is the pygmy shrew at 1,200 beats per minute. That's about 15 times faster than an average person's resting heart rate!

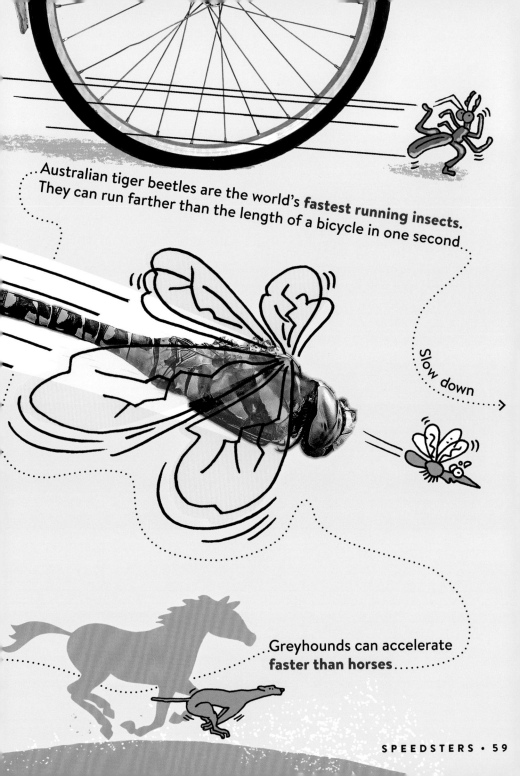

Australian tiger beetles are the world's **fastest running insects.** They can run farther than the length of a bicycle in one second.

Slow down

Greyhounds can accelerate **faster than horses.**

It can take up to a **whole month** for a sloth to digest its food.

Moving at a snail's pace means covering a litt

Sunflower sea stars have **15,000 feet** but can travel only about the length of three guitars in one minute.

At its top speed, a banana slug takes one minute to cover the length of a banana.

ore than the length of a skateboard in an hour.

Cool coral

Most **coral larvae** travel no more than a mile (1.6km) from their parents, take root on the ocean floor, and never move again.

Fast-growing staghorn coral grow at about the same speed as human hair

Pygmy seahorses—which are smaller than a paper clip—spend their entire lives attached to coral. As babies, they grow bumps to match their habitat

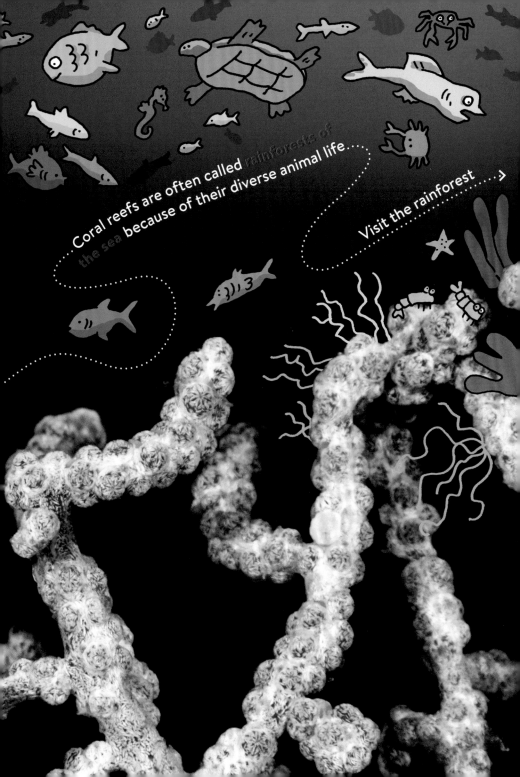

Coral reefs are often called rainforests of the sea because of their diverse animal life.

Visit the rainforest....›

Rainforest-dwelling **happy face spiders** can have a pattern that looks like a smiling face on their bodies.

Each blue poison frog has a unique spot pattern on its back. No two of these rainforest frogs have the same print

Hop this way

Facing each other and opening up their **jaws** as wide as they can is how male **hippopotamuses** size each other up before a fight.

The **throat** of a moray eel contains a second set of **jaws**.

While they are in the water, **hippopotamuses** are often followed by barbel fish, which nibble parasites off the hippos' skin, clean inside their mouths, and even eat their **poop**!

A frog uses its eyes to help push food down its **throat**.

The northern Pinocchio tree frog gets its name from its long "**nose**"—a fleshy spike that sticks out from its **head**.

A star-nosed mole finds **prey** using the 22 tentacles around its **nose**.

A full-grown male ostrich is tall enough for its **head** to reach the **bottom** of the net on an NBA basketball hoop.

The olm, a type of blind salamander that lives at the **bottom** of underwater **caves**, can survive 10 years without eating.

Sloths eat the **green** algae that grow on their fur.

Green herons **drop** insects in water as bait to attract fish.

When it's time to **poop**, a three-toed **sloth** typically goes underneath the same tree each time. Scientists think it may help them communicate with other sloths... or fertilize trees they like.

Egyptian vultures **drop** stones on ostrich eggs to **crack** them open.

Sea otters store a rock under their armpits to **crack** open **prey**, like clams.

Armor up!

Hanging from **cave** ceilings in Venezuela, giant **centipedes** prey on bats.

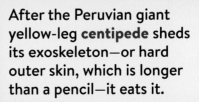

After the Peruvian giant yellow-leg **centipede** sheds its exoskeleton—or hard outer skin, which is longer than a pencil—it eats it.

...>............An ironclad beetle's exoskeleton
is so strong it can survive being

run over
by a car

Bug out over beetles

Go to page 152

.....*Glyptodon*, an extinct relative of the armadillo with a **spiky club-shaped tail**, was so well covered in armor that even saber-toothed cats had a hard time attacking it.....

Back in time .....>

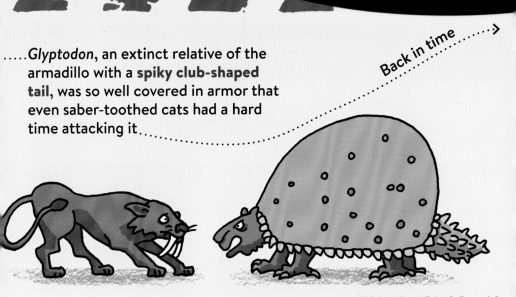

Giant ground sloths, which lived more than 13,000 years ago, **ate AVOCADOS** whole.

Edestus, a type of shark that had arcs of teeth on the roof and floor of its mouth, sliced through fish like a pair of scissors.

The dawn horse, the first known horse, was the size of a small dog...

A near-perfect woolly mammoth baby was found in Russia after being frozen for 40,000 years.

Chill out

Trot on over

Go to page 128

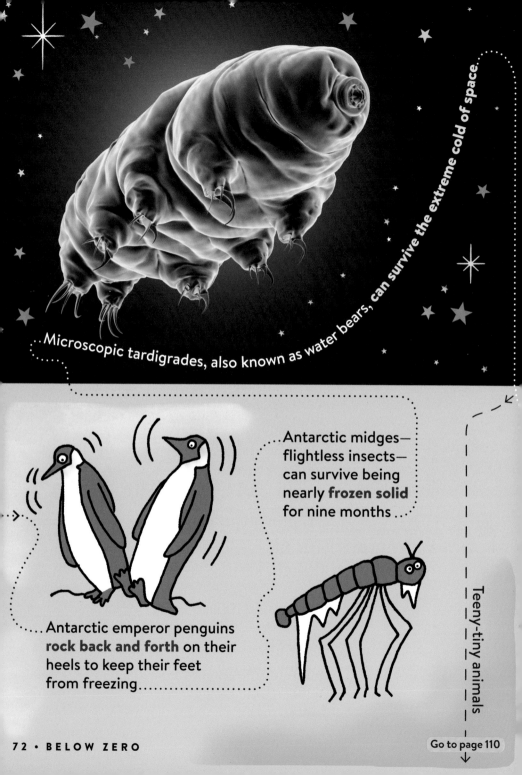

Microscopic tardigrades, also known as water bears, can survive the extreme cold of space.

Antarctic midges—flightless insects—can survive being nearly **frozen solid** for nine months

Antarctic emperor penguins **rock back and forth** on their heels to keep their feet from freezing

Teeny-tiny animals

Go to page 110

Arctic ground squirrels drop their body temperature down to below freezing while they are in a state of

HIBERNATION.

Time for a snooze

.....To keep warm in Arctic waters, beluga whales have a **layer of blubber** as thick as 10 slices of bread.............

Even when they're in a deep hibernation-like sleep, called torpor, Australia's eastern pygmy possums can sense danger, such as a wildfire

Down under

More kangaroos than humans live in Australia

The shell of Australia's giant panda snail can grow to be as large as a tennis ball.

An echidna lays a **tiny egg** the size of a grape, then keeps it in a pouch on its belly.

Crack open more

Prairie chickens, a grassland animal, lay their eggs on n

Horn sharks produce **spiral-shaped eggs**, which they screw into rocks and crevices with their mouths

es called **booming grounds**, named after the low noise the male birds make...

Great grasslands

Skates, a type of fish related to rays, have **ravioli-shaped** egg cases ......

Zebras, which live in the grasslands of eastern and southern Africa, **pass gas** when they get startled.

Leopards sometimes carry their food high up in a tree to avoid it being stolen by other big cats or hyenas...

On the prowl

Cats have whiskers on the backs of their front legs.

Most cats aren't wild about water, but tigers are excellent swimmers and regularly take dips to cool off.

A jaguar's powerful jaws can crack a turtle's shell

Talk about turtles

Go to page 168

Félicette, a stray cat from France, was launched into space in 1963 for a 15-minute mission. Then her capsule slowly parachuted safely back to Earth...

Blast off!

Male cats are more likely to be left-pawed, and females are more likely to be right-pawed.

The Manatee Nebula, a giant cloud of gas and dust in space, got its name because it looks like a manatee floating on its back with its flippers crossed over its belly.

In the night sky, there are more dogs represented in the constellations than cats...

Harbor seals are capable of using guide stars, called lodestars, to help them find their way when they're swimming far from shore...

Dive in

A penguin's **BLACK-AND-WHITE "TUXEDO"** helps it camouflage while swimming—its white belly blends with the sky when viewed from below, and its black back blends with dark water when viewed from above.

Look carefully

By staying very still and using their bumpy skin as camouflage, alligators ca

...sguise themselves as floating logs when swimming in **swamps and wetlands**

Wild wetlands →

Cuttlefish match not only the color of their surroundings, but also the texture, like the rocky ocean floor.

Swamp rabbits are excellent swimmers. They jump in the water to escape predators and dive to find food

Go to page 86

Swim over

...Like the hippo, the capybara—a relative of the guinea pig—has its eyes, ears, and nose located high on its head, letting it peek above water while the rest of its body remains hidden ...

Sitatunga, swamp-dwelling antelopes, have **banana-shaped hooves** that keep them from slipping in the mud.

River otters sometimes slide down muddy hillsides for fun

Prepare for more mud

Beavers have an extra set of clear eyelids so they can **see underwater** when swimming in murky rivers, marshes, and wetlands

Mudpuppies, a type of salamander that lives on the muddy bottoms of rivers and ponds, can make a sound that resembles a **barking dog**

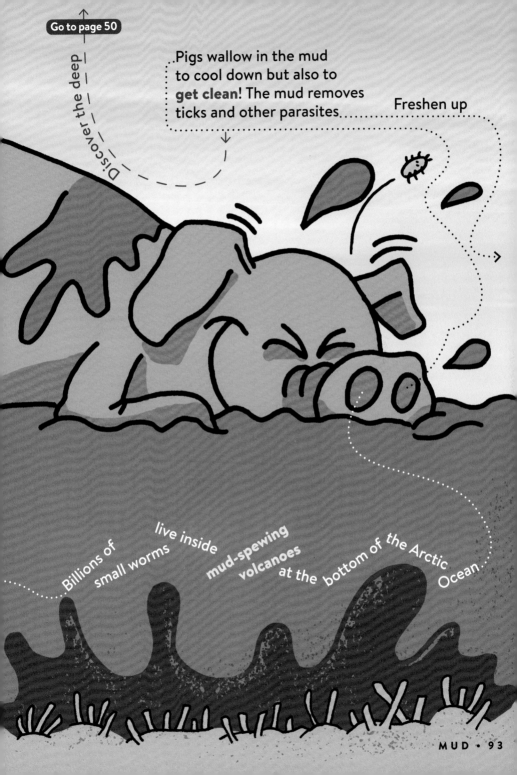

Go to page 50

Discover the deep

Pigs wallow in the mud to cool down but also to **get clean**! The mud removes ticks and other parasites.

Freshen up

Billions of small worms live inside **mud-spewing volcanoes** at the bottom of the Arctic Ocean.

Go to page 54

Monkey mania

Apes and monkeys pick lice out of each other's fur and eat them

Japanese snow monkeys sometimes take baths in **hot springs**

Go to page 180

Get more goo

It's getting hairy

Cats lick their fur to stay clean, but also to cool down.

Red and gray kangaroos prefer to eat and groom themselves with their left paws.

The babies of some bird species create a fecal sac, which is a case around their own poop. Their parents clean out these bird "diapers" from the nest regularly by either dropping the sacs off somewhere else... or by eating them

The fur on a fennec fox's feet protects them from the desert's **hot sand**.

Female snow leopards **line their dens with their own fur** to keep their cubs warm.

Zebras that live in warmer climates have **more stripes**, which scientists think might keep them cooler.

Head home

Go to page 178

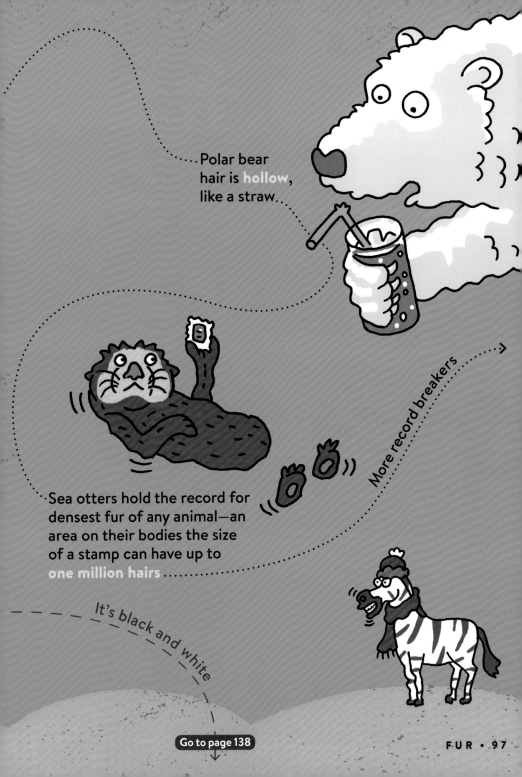

Polar bear hair is **hollow**, like a straw.

Sea otters hold the record for densest fur of any animal—an area on their bodies the size of a stamp can have up to **one million hairs**

More record breakers

It's black and white

Go to page 138

...The world's **loudest**

PURR

by a domestic cat measured as loud as a vacuum cleaner.........

Polar bears have the largest paws of all bears—they're as wide as a **Frisbee**.....

More head turners

A Texas longhorn steer, a type of cow, set a world record for having horns that span **wider than the Statue of Liberty's head**

Hearing things?

Go to page 12

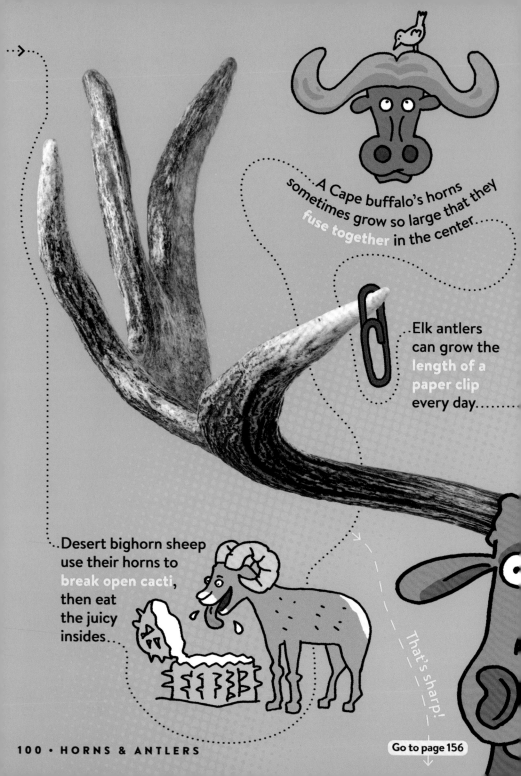

A Cape buffalo's horns sometimes grow so large that they **fuse together** in the center.

Elk antlers can grow the **length of a paper clip every day.**

Desert bighorn sheep use their horns to **break open cacti,** then eat the juicy insides.

That's sharp!

Go to page 156

Kosmoceratops richardsoni, a dinosaur that lived 76 million years ago, had **15 horns**— more than any other animal.

Flutter this way

The **horn moth** lays its eggs in the horns of dead animals. When they hatch, the larvae then feast on the bone.

When African plated lizards are threatened, they hide in the **grooves** of rocks, then inflate their bodies by filling their **lungs** with air, wedging them so tight nothing can pull them out.

A sloth has special tissues that "tape" its **lungs** to its rib cage so it can breathe while hanging **upside down**.

Desert tortoises dig **grooves** in the ground to collect rainwater.

The white-lined sphinx moth caterpillar, an animal that lives in the **desert**, sometimes raises its head when it's startled and resembles an Egyptian sphinx.

Velociraptors, turkey-size **dinosaurs**, could **leap** higher than a soccer goalpost.

Opossum babies can hang **upside down** from tree branches by their **tails** for short periods of time.

The giraffe has the longest **tail** of any **land animal**— it's as long as a golf club!

The largest **land animal** believed to have ever lived was *Patagotitan mayorum*, a plant-eating **dinosaur** that weighed almost as much as a commercial jet filled with fuel and cargo.

Get to work!

Scientists think the **leaps** and spins that spinner dolphins perform in the air let fellow **dolphins** know where they're going or if danger is ahead.

The United States Navy trains bottlenose **dolphins** and sea lions to find and retrieve equipment lost at sea.

...>.....The **"chief mouser"** is a cat whose job is to catch rodents at the British prime minister's house ....

.....African giant pouched rats are **incredibly intelligent**— they can be trained to sniff out explosives and even some diseases.........

At a golf course in Oregon, you can **hire a goat to be your caddie**. The goat will carry golf clubs and balls in a special pack on its back

Off to the farm

Dozens of goats, sheep, and donkeys are used to keep the grass trimme

...Cows spend about eight hours a day chewing their cud—grass that they have already eaten once and regurgitated to eat again...

Munch on this ·····>

* an airport in Chicago, Illinois ·····

Dolphins use their teeth to **hold on to fish**, not to chew them—they swallow their food whole

Beavers have

orange teeth.

Megalodon, a type of shark that went extinct more than two million years ago, had teeth **as long as butter knives**.

Instead of teeth, **microscopic tardigrades** have two daggerlike mouthparts called stylets that they use to pierce their prey and drink their insides.

Look closely

Some monkeys **floss** using bird feathers

Blast into the past

Go to page 70

An average bed has up to

1.5 million dust mites

living in it

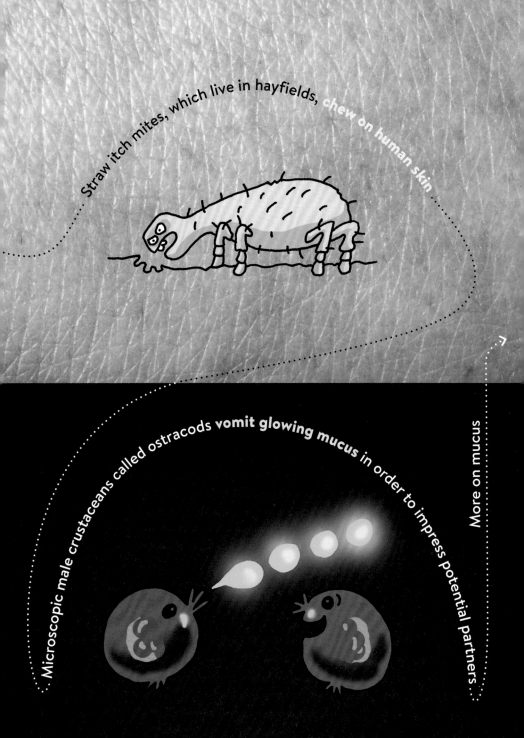

Straw itch mites, which live in hayfields, chew on human skin

Microscopic male crustaceans called ostracods vomit glowing mucus in order to impress potential partners

More on mucus

When whales clear their blowholes, they spew out air, water, and whale snot.

Go to page 36

Wild about whales

Bonobo moms suck the snot out of their *babies' noses*

Notable noses

When stressed, spadefoot toads release a substance that smells like peanut butter.

When **honeybees sting**, they send a message to the rest of the hive by producing an odor that smells like bananas.

Create a buzz

Honey badgers, which like to eat honey and bee larvae, have such thick skin they can withstand the **venomous** stings of African bees.

In their lifetime, a group of 12 honeybees will produce one teaspoon of honey.

Venomous black mamba snakes sleep in empty termite mounds.

Cassowaries are large, flightless birds with sharp 4-inch-long (10cm-long) talons which they use to slice open predators with a powerful **kick**.

A sea lamprey latches onto fish with its suction-cup **mouth**, then scrapes off their flesh with its sharp teeth so it can feast on their blood.

Spiders' feet are covered in millions of tiny **hairs** designed to help them cling to any surface.

Male kangaroos fight rivals by balancing on their tails so they can **kick** with both of their feet.

Dolphins are born with just a few **hairs** around their snouts—these whiskers can look like a mustache.

After biting their victims—which are usually cows and horses—vampire bats use their **tongues** to lick up the blood.

Giant anteaters break into **termite mounds** and anthills and use their sticky **tongues** to lick up 35,000 termites and ants in a day.

A lick to the eyeball helps a **gecko** keep its eyes clean.

From head to **tail**, the yellow bullhead catfish is covered in over 175,000 tastebuds, 20 times more than humans have in their **mouths**.

Sometimes when a **gecko** loses its **tail**, it will come back to eat it!

Grrrrowl

When they're getting ready to hibernate, grizzly bears' main priority is eating fatty **foods**. Sometimes, they'll eat the fatty belly and eyeballs of a fish and leave the rest!

Walruses use their whiskers to search for **food** on the ocean floor.

Go to page 34

Take a snooze

Sun bears sometimes walk on their hind legs while **carrying their babies** in their arms.

A woman in Virginia found a black bear **taking a nap in a kiddie pool** in her backyard.

Pizzly bears are a rare **hybrid** of polar and grizzly bears.

Walk this way →

Brown bears **communicate with each other through their feet**! They release a scent from glands on their feet by twisting their paws in the ground in a little dance.

A giant panda can eat up to **84 pounds (38kg) of bamboo a day**—that's the same weight as 336 hamburgers!

When camels' **leathery foot pads** hit the ground, they spread out to keep from sinking into the sand.

Geckoes are able to change the stickiness of their feet—they can turn it on and off.

The largest known **fossilized dinosaur footprint** ever discovered was about the size of a large bathtub.

Dig up more fossils

A 66-million-year-old fossil was nicknamed **"crazy beast"** by scientists because of its strange features: It had front teeth like a rodent, back legs that splayed out like a crocodile, and a hole on top of its snout

Just imagine

Scientists believe fossils of extinct animals like dinosaurs inspired ancient people around the world to believe in **mythical creatures**, such as dragons.

As late as the 16th century, traders brought narwhal tusks from North America and Russia to Europe and claimed they were

UNICORN HORNS

Hooray for horns

Go to page 100

Giant oarfish can grow to be longer than a pickup truck. They're thought to be the inspiration for tales about **sea serpents**.

No horsing around

In prehistoric Egypt, flamingos that laid eggs on hot salt flats may have been the inspiration for the **phoenix**—a bird that dies by burning up and then is born again from the ashes.

Stories of the **kraken**—a massive sea monster—originated in Scandinavian folklore. The Old Norse words *at kraka* mean to drag downward, which is what tales said the creature did to ships with its giant arms.

The unicorn is the **official national animal of Scotland**.

Until 1976, taxi drivers in London, Englan

...ere required by law to have food on hand for their horses—even though horse-and-buggy taxis were a thing of the past.

And the winner is

Legendary racehorse

SECRETARIAT

had a heart more than twice as big as the one in an average horse.

...A horse makes enough saliva to fill up 100 soda cans every day.

...A bulldog named Tillman became famous for being able to

ride a skateboard

by pushing off the ground with his paw, which is how he cruised around parks and even New York City's Times Square...

Woof!

To collect **water** and keep their skin moist, Australian green tree **frogs** create their own fog. They jump from the cool night air to their warm underground burrows, creating moisture.

The neon flying squid can propel itself out of the **ocean** at speeds almost as fast as the world's fastest man, Usain Bolt, can **run**.

When trumpeter swans **run** across the **water** to take flight, it sounds like galloping horses.

When boxer dogs get **excited**, they sometimes "box" each other with their front paws while balancing on their back legs.

Excited guinea pigs sometimes "popcorn"—the name for when they **jump** straight up in the air.

Hairy frogfish aren't **frogs** and they don't have hair—they're a fish covered in fleshy spines that walk on the seafloor with their fins!

The giant bumphead parrotfish uses its oversize forehead to **bump** into rivals near **ocean** coral reefs.

If an alligator is in a Florida manatee's space, the manatee often **swims** up to it and **bumps** it until it moves out of the way.

The water opossum has a watertight **pouch** that keeps its babies dry while it **swims** in streams and ponds.

When a young wallaby senses danger, it often **jumps** into its mother's **pouch** for protection.

One species of batfish
looks like it's wearing
bright-red lipstick
on its mouth

Blue tang fish are also known as **palette tang** because their black markings resemble an artist's palette.

There's a pattern here

A jaguar's spots are called **rosettes** because the jagged circles on its coat resemble roses.

Male white-spotted pufferfish impress females by creating patterns on the seafloor and then decorating them with shells

Computer scientists created a **barcode-like scanning system** that identifies individual zebras from a photograph............................ In black and white ⟩

ISBN 978-1-913750-73-2

Giant pandas
sometimes do

H
A
N
D

S
T
A
N
D
S

when they pee.

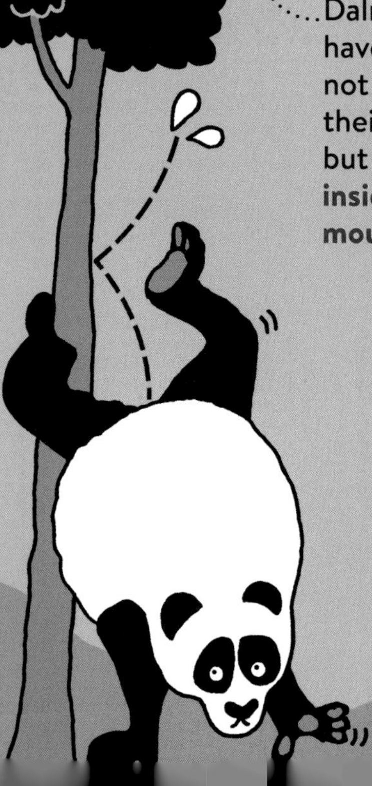

...Dalmatians
have spots
not only on
their coats,
but also
**inside their
mouths**......

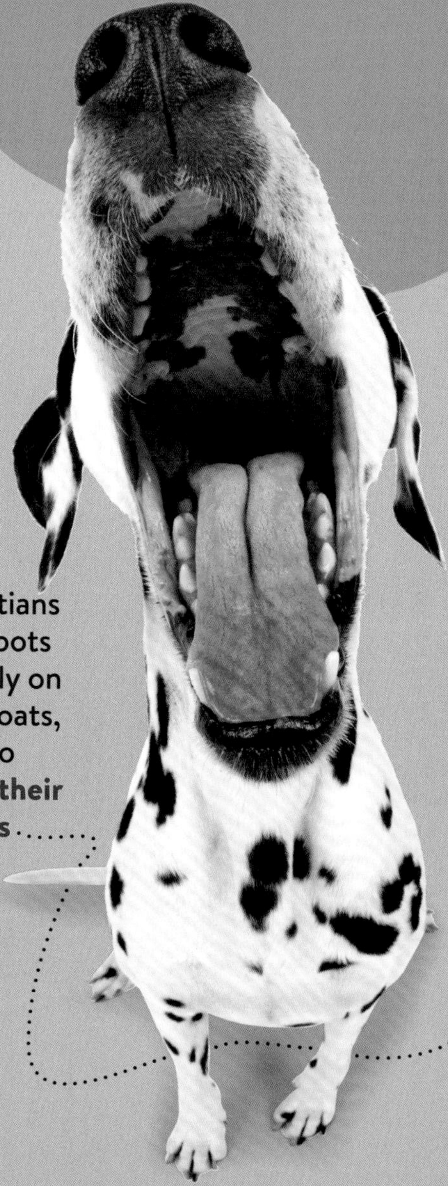

When **orcas** are born, their bellies and eye patches are pinkish-orange, not white.

A group of penguins on land is called a
WADDLE

BALD-FACED HORNETS CAN BUILD NESTS BIGGER THAN BASKETBALLS.

That stings!

Tarantula hawks aren't spiders or birds; they're wasps that have one of the insect world's **most painful stings**..

Scorpions duel with their venomous tails; the winner stings and eats its rival......

More venom

Venom from spitting cobra snakes can spray longer than the length of a hockey stick.

The world's smallest bird egg, laid by the vervain hummingbird, is the size of a pea.

King cobras are the only snakes that build nests for their eggs.

Galápagos penguins lay their eggs in holes found in lava rocks.

Badgers dig shallow holes outside of their dens to use as toilets.

Black herons fold their feathers over their heads to form a makeshift umbrella that creates shade to attract fish in shallow water.

Alligators swallow small rocks to help them stay underwater longer.

Moose dive underwater to eat plants off the bottom of lakes and ponds.

Platypuses search for food at the bottom of ponds and rivers using their supersensitive bills, which can pick up the electric fields produced by their prey.

Ruby-throated hummingbirds flap their wings more than 50 times in one second.

The wings of pterosaurs—flying reptiles that lived at the time of dinosaurs—were not only for flying: They also used them for walking on the ground.

The dinosaur *Spinosaurus* hunted for prey both in the water and on the shoreline like modern-day herons.

Inside its stomach, a ghost crab has teeth that not only help it digest food, but when ground together, also make a growling noise it uses to scare off predators.

A brown pelican can hold three times more food in its bill than in its stomach.

One species of crab, called the coconut crab, uses its serrated front claws like a knife to crack open whole coconuts.

Sidestep this way ·········>

Despite their name, **hermit crabs** are social and can gather and live in groups of more than 100 in the wild ...

Go to page 172

Female pea crabs spend their entire adult lives **inside of an oyster, mussel, or scallop shell**

If a fiddler crab **loses its claw** in a fight or attack, it grows a new one

A 35-foot-long (11m-long) lobster statue greets people entering Shediac, New Brunswick, Canada, also known as the "lobster capital of the world"

Grow it again

Get artsy

FACTON

In 2008, a French artist made **1,600** papier-mâché giant pandas, one for every panda left in the wild at the time, and displayed them in cities around the world

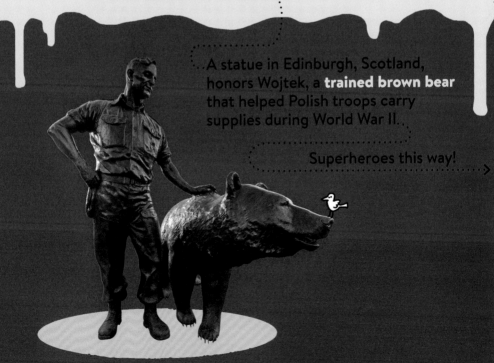

You can buy **paintings** created by a red panda, rhino, or cheetah at a zoo in Houston, Texas

A statue in Edinburgh, Scotland, honors Wojtek, a **trained brown bear** that helped Polish troops carry supplies during World War II.

Superheroes this way!

An Australian tabby cat named Sally was credited with **saving her owner's life** from a house fire by jumping on him while he was sleeping and meowing loudly, waking him up

Frida, a yellow Labrador retriever, **helped rescue survivors** after an earthquake in Mexico

Soldiers in World War I used glass jars to gather

glowworms

which emitted enough light to read maps and reports at night

On the bright side ›

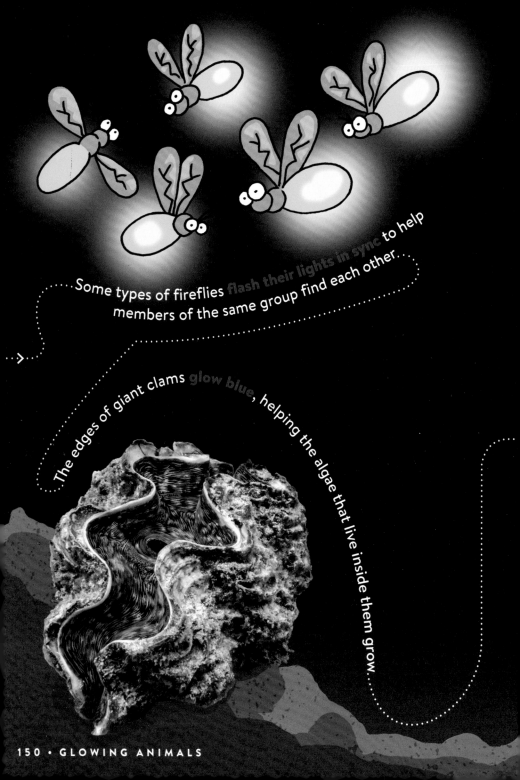

Some types of fireflies *flash their lights in sync* to help members of the same group find each other.

The edges of giant clams *glow blue*, helping the algae that live inside them grow

Go to page 88

Hide over here

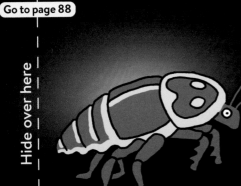

One species of cockroach glows green to trick predators into thinking it's a toxic type of beetle.....

More creepy-crawlies

Hawaiian bobtail squid camouflage themselves at night by glowing blue and mimicking the moonlight.................

When under attack, brittle stars will detach one of their glowing arms so predators will follow it, while they make a quick escape...........

The titan beetle can **bite** a pencil in half with its jaws

The Namib Desert beetle survives in the extremely hot and dry desert by collecting water droplets from the air on its bumpy shell. Scientists are studying the beetle to develop a water bottle that could capture moisture from the air and refill itself.

Off to the future

Go to page 96

Scientists copied the patterns of beaver and sea otter hair to design material for a new warm,

FURRY WET SUIT.

Fabulous fur

Inspired by an elephant's trunk, scientists invented a flexible robot

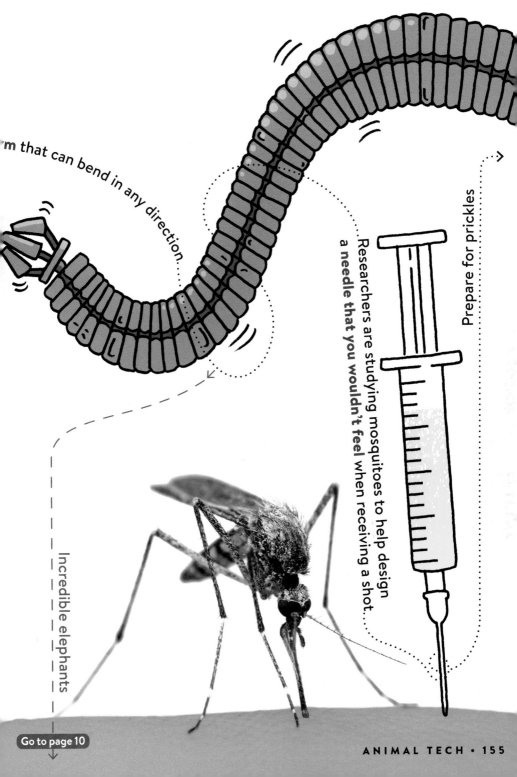

...m that can bend in any direction.

Prepare for prickles

Researchers are studying mosquitoes to help design a needle that you wouldn't feel when receiving a shot.

Incredible elephants

Go to page 10

Go to page 30

Lots of lizards

Baby hedgehogs are born with soft spines. After just a day, the spines become hard and sharp.

Texas horned lizards can inflate themselves with air so the spikes that cover their bodies poke out, making it hard for a predator to eat them.

Porcupines rattle hollow quills at the base of their tails to warn predators to back off.

The puss caterpillar's "hairs" are actually tiny hollow spines filled with venom.

The elf owl, **the world's smallest owl**, makes its home inside holes of spiky desert saguaro cactuses.

For something a little softer

Franchesca, an English Angora rabbit, **set a world record** by having fur that was just over 14 inches (36cm), the longest of any rabbit.

In the winter, Arctic foxes sleep with their fluffy tails **wrapped around their bodies for warmth.**

An alpaca's **soft wool**, which is shaved to make yarn, is fire-resistant.

Go to page 94

Time to clean up

When squirrels fall, they fluff out their

BUSHY TAILS

for a slower, softer landing.

More rodents

To keep their thick coats clean, South American chinchillas take **baths in fine volcanic dust.**

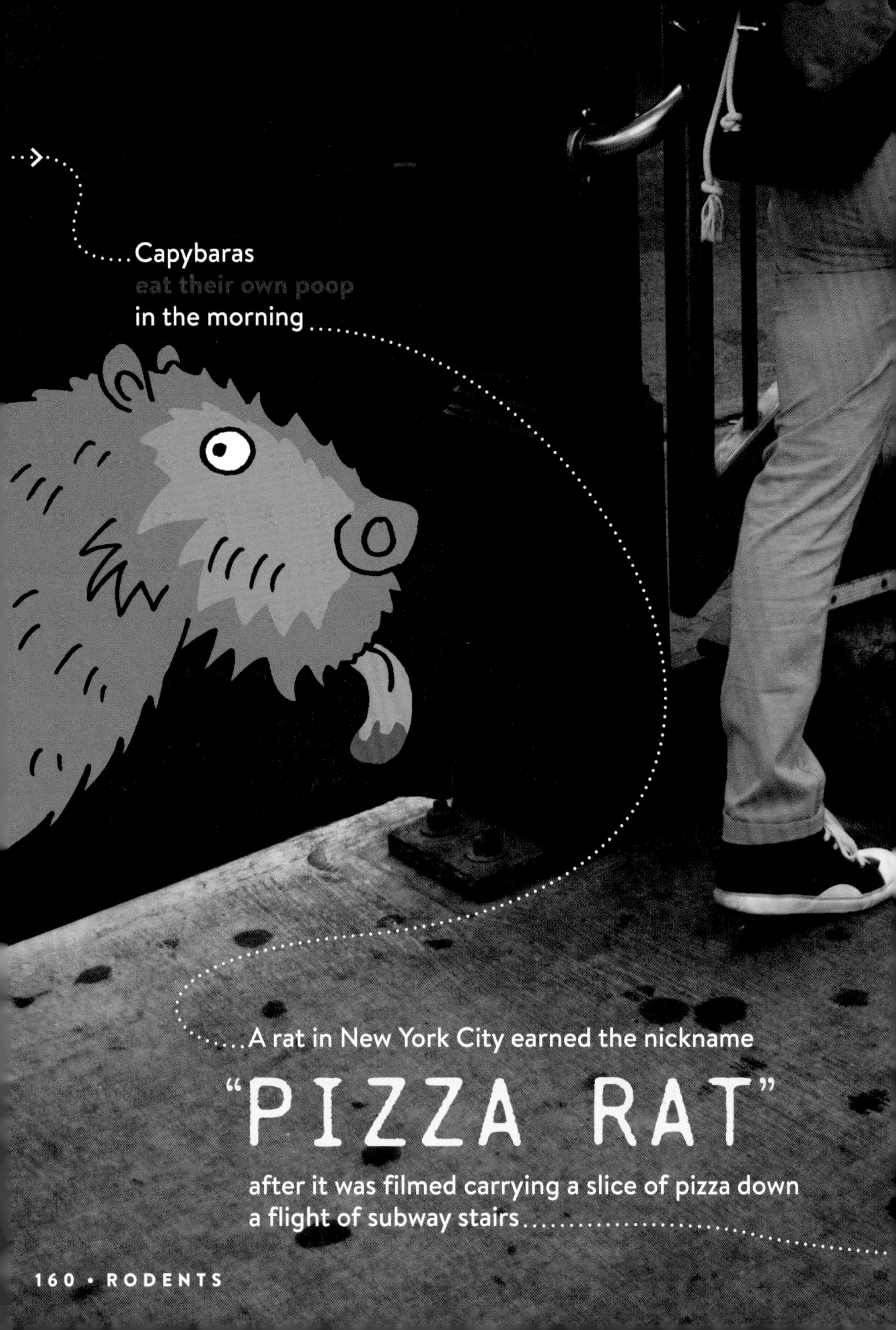

Capybaras
eat their own poop
in the morning

...A rat in New York City earned the nickname

"PIZZA RAT"

after it was filmed carrying a slice of pizza down
a flight of subway stairs.......

Scurry to the subway ⟩

Koalas cool down by hugging **trees**.

Each wolf **pack** has a **unique** howl.

Some animals have **unique** fingerprints, just like humans—including gorillas, chimpanzees, and **koalas**.

In New York City, two goats wandering along the subway tracks held up commuters for over an **hour**.

The pygmy shrew has to eat every **hour** or it will **die**.

Eastern hognose snakes pretend to **die** when **attacked** by a predator, becoming stiff and lifeless, even when poked.

A beaver cuts down an average of 300 trees in a year.

Swim down the river

Hyenas vomit around their dens and caves... then other members of their pack roll in it.

A camel's spit is mostly vomit, not saliva.

When attacked, Sally Lightfoot crabs spit water at predators.

When threatened, river otters make a **screaming sound** that can be heard 1.5 miles (2.4km) away.

Amazon river dolphins have been observed doing a "trophy lift"—**lifting live turtles above the water** to impress females.

...A red-bellied piranha gets most of its food by nipping at the tails of larger fish in South American rivers...

The Greeks named the hippopotamus *ippopótamos*—or "river horse"—because of the amount of time the animals spend in the water.

Saltwater crocodiles live in both freshwater rivers and the ocean. They even scavenge for food alongside sharks.....

Surf's up

Cowries, the shells of mollusks, were **once used as money**

African penguins sometimes dig nests on top of **piles of their own poop** on beaches near Cape Town, South Africa

Whether a **sea turtle** is a male or female depends on the temperature of the sand where its mother laid her eggs

Turtle-y awesome

Western painted turtles can hold their breath for four months......

A jellyfish-like parasite that lives in the flesh of Chinook salmon is the only animal that doesn't need any oxygen to survive.

Mosquito larvae live underwater—but breathe air through a special snorkel-like tube.

Male walruses have **air sacs in their necks** that act like floatation devices so they don't sink as easily

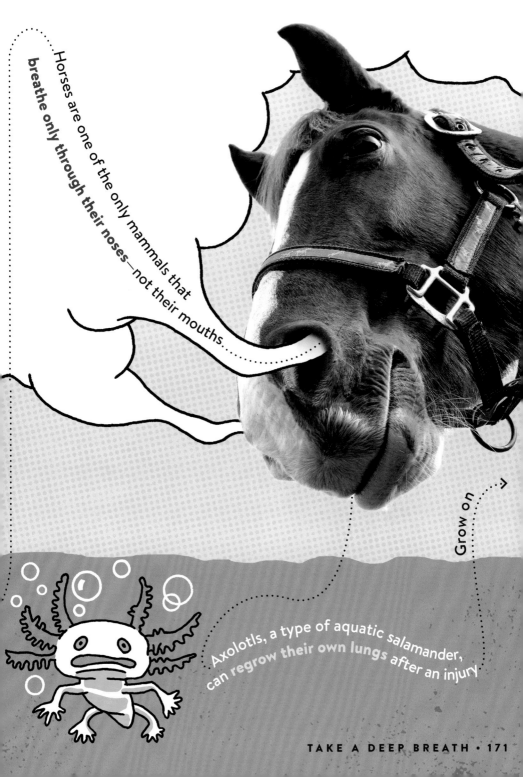

Horses are one of the only mammals that breathe only through their noses—not their mouths.

Grow on

Axolotls, a type of aquatic salamander, can regrow their own lungs after an injury

... If their bodies become infected with parasites, some types of sea slugs will chop off their own heads, leave their old bodies behind, and **regrow new healthy bodies**......

Some types of

sea stars

can grow an entire body from a lost limb...

Extraordinary extremities ......

Cats can spring up to nine times their **height** from a sitting position.

The spine of a cheetah is more **flexible** than those of other big **cats**, allowing it to cover the length of a pickup truck with each stride.

Brittle stars have arms that are **flexible** and about as long as a tennis racket.

When standing, the world's tallest dog—a Great Dane named Zeus—stood at the same **height** as two stacked emperor **penguins**.

A **seahorse** can use its tail to hold onto **grasses** so it doesn't get swept away in the ocean current.

To help lead her cubs through the savanna's tall **grasses**, an African lion mother raises her black tufted **tail** like a flag.

The **tails** of spider **monkey** babies act like seat belts. To keep from falling, they wrap their tails around their mothers while swinging through trees.

Capuchin **monkeys** in Venezuela rub **millipedes** on their fur because millipedes have special chemicals in them that keep insects away.

Humboldt **penguins** shoot "**poop** bombs" that can fly more than 4 feet (1.2m) away.

Every year, a single sea cucumber generates 30 pounds (14kg) of **poop**, which it **drops** on coral reefs, keeping them healthy.

When viewed from **above**, Isabela Island in the Galápagos looks like a **seahorse**.

Australian pranksters will often jokingly warn tourists about vicious koala bears that may **drop** on them from **above**.

How smart ------------------------>

Yellow-spotted **millipedes** release a chemical that **smells** like toasted almonds when under attack.

Ken Allen, a young **orangutan** at a zoo in California, sometimes unscrewed the bolts of his enclosure, walked around his nursery at night, then locked himself back in before zookeepers noticed.

Even though some say this fruit **smells** like onion and gym socks, durian is one of the **orangutan**'s favorite foods.

Honeybees can solve simple addition and subtraction problems.

New Caledonian crows carve hooks on t[

Go to page 16

Fly this way

d of sticks to grab grubs better...

Construction ahead

Pocket gophers use stones like shovels to build their burrows...

Some birds use **snakeskin** when building their nests.

Arctic foxes grow **colorful "gardens"** around their dens in the tundra thanks to their poop and urine—which make a rich compost for plants.

The ovenbird get its name from the shape of its nest, which looks like an **outdoor bread oven.**

Paper wasps build nests by gathering wood and bits of plants, chewing them, then **spitting out the pulp**, which dries to form a paperlike product

More gooey stuff ⟶

Prairie dogs build **special rooms in their burrows** that they use as nurseries and even bathrooms!

After licking an object that smells new to them, hedgehogs may produce a **frothy foam** from their saliva and put it all over their bodies, including their spines.

Slugs and snails communicate through the chemicals they leave

Tarsiers, a type of primate, communicate with each other through a **high-pitched screech** that predators and humans can't hear.

Koko, a western lowland gorilla, learned **1,000 words** in American Sign Language...

Scientists are using **paw-activated buttons** that sound out words to study whether dogs and cats can "talk" with humans.......

Perfect paws

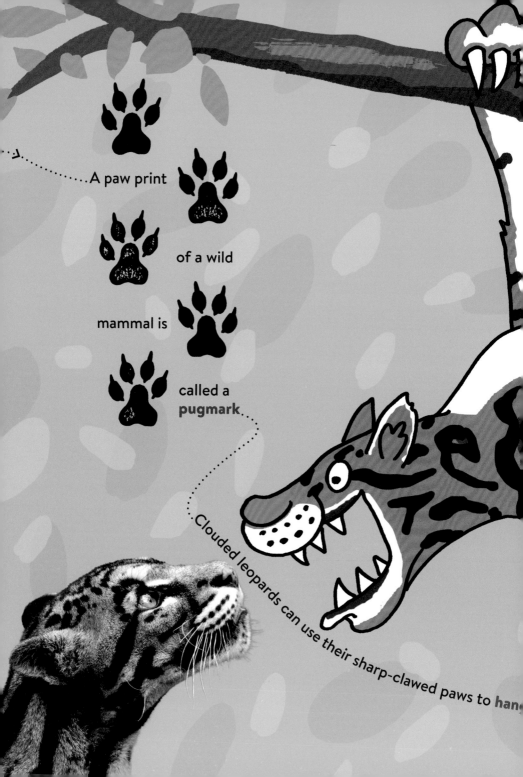

A paw print

of a wild

mammal is

called a **pugmark**

Clouded leopards can use their sharp-clawed paws to hang

Hang on

...side down from branches.

The **upside-down jelly**—which looks like a plant—rests its main body, or bell, on the seafloor and waves its underbelly up toward the sun to catch food floating by.

The sucker-footed bat is one of the rare bats that don't sleep upside-down—it produces a sweat-like substance to **stick upright** on leaves.

That's a sticky situation

Hop to it

A **frog's tongue**

isn't sticky—its spit is! When the saliva makes contact with prey—like a fly—it becomes a thin liquid and spreads over the bug, then immediately thickens up, helping the frog keep its grip.

frog babies in here

The **waxy monkey frog** makes a waxlike substance that it rubs all over its body to keep from drying out in the sun...

The marsupial frog has a **pouch like a kangaroo's** on its back, and it carries its eggs in there until they develop into froglets...

The rainforest-dwelling strawberry poison frog is red all over except for its **bright blue legs**—the source of its nickname, the "blue jeans" frog...

When a Budgett's frog is disturbed, it lets out a **shrill scream**

Get loud!

Some frogs lay their eggs on the undersides of leaves that hang over streams and rivers. When they hatch, the tadpoles *plop into the water*.

Explore the rainforest

Go to page 64

Screech owls have a unique way of keeping parasitic insects off their **babies**: They capture wormlike snakes and leave them in the nest to eat the parasites that would otherwise infest the owlets.

Naked mole-rats live in communities ruled by one dominant female; all the other family members take care of her **babies** and even eat her **poop**!

A giraffe's **legs** and **neck** are the same length.

Ants don't have ears—they listen by feeling vibrations with their **legs**.

The giraffe weevils has an extra-long **neck** that it uses like a crane to build a leaf nest for a single **egg**.

During the American Civil War, bat **poop** was collected from **Bracken Cave** in Texas to make gunpowder.

At **Bracken Cave** in the **summer**, newborn baby bats cram together to roost in groups of as many 500 per square foot.

More proud papas

Antarctica is the only continent that doesn't have any native **ant** species.

During the **summer**, a colony of 3,000 gentoo penguins takes up residence outside "Penguin Post Office" in **Antarctica**, the southernmost post office in the world.

After female giant water bugs lay their **eggs**, the males carry the eggs on their backs until they hatch.

...Male Darwin's frogs swallow developing tadpoles for two months while they grow, then cough them out when they are frogs...

...Ostrich moms and dads take turns sitting on their eggs—males take the night shift because their dark feathers make them harder for predators to see...

Seahorse dads are the ones that carry the eggs and give birth to bab

It's getting dark

Go to page 22

Brothers and sisters ·······>

·······ahorses—up to *2,000 at a time!*

ANIMAL DADS · 195

...>.....When walking through their underground tunnels, **naked mole-rats** have to make way for their older siblings.

To make sure no one gets lost, shrew siblings make a chain behind their mother.

... Nine-banded armadillo mothers almost always give birth to **identical quadruplets**........

...ach biting on to one another...

They grow up so fast!

When sand tiger sharks are growing inside their mother, they **eat their brothers and sisters** until there is usually just one left.

When cheetah cubs are old enough to head out on their own, the male siblings typically live in a group called a **coalition**...

The world's longest-living land animal is

Jonathan,

a tortoise that was born before
the first gasoline car was
even invented!

Index

hairy frogfish 133
happy face spiders 64
harbor seals 85
Hawaiian bobtail squid 151
Hawaiian monk seals 28
heart 58, 129
hedgehogs 156, 180
hermit crabs 144
heroes 147–9
herons 67, 142
hibernation 14, 34, 73–5
high-altitude animals 47–9
hippopotamuses 15, 66, 165
honey badgers 118
honeybees 117, 118, 176
horned lizards 156
hornets 139
horn moths 101
horns 14, 99–101
horn sharks 78
horses 71, 128–9, 171
horseshoe crabs 186
Humboldt penguins 175
hummingbirds 142–3
humpback whales 37
hydrothermal vents 50
hyenas 163

iguanas 29
intelligence 176–7
ironclad beetles 68

jaguars 56–7, 82, 136
Japanese snow monkeys 94
jaws 66, 82
jellyfish 186
jobs for animals 103–5

jumping 102, 103, 132, 133, 174

kangaroos 76, 95, 118
king cobras 142
koalas 162, 175
Komodo dragons 30
Kosmoceratops richardsoni 101
kraken 127

Labrador retrievers 149
lampreys 118
lanternfish 14
leaping 102, 103, 132, 133, 174
legs 6, 46, 82, 192
lemurs 14, 27
leopards 26, 40, 52, 81, 96, 184–5
lice 94
lightning bugs (fireflies) 14, 150
lions 32–3, 174
little brown bats 22
lizards 29–31, 41, 43, 102, 119, 123, 156
lobsters 145
longhorn steer 99
lungs 48, 102, 168–71
lynx 52

mammoths 71
manatees 15, 84, 133
mantises 43
marine iguanas 29
marine slugs 15
marine snow 51
marsupial frogs 190

meerkats 34
Megalodon 108
mice 40, 48
microscopic animals 72, 109–11
midges 72
millipedes 174, 175
mites 110, 111
moles 66, 115
monarch butterflies 18–19
monkeys 53–5, 94, 109, 174
moose 15, 142
moray eels 66
mosquitoes 155, 170
moths 101, 102
mucus 111–13
mud 92–3
mudpuppies 92
mythical creatures 125–7

naked mole-rats 192, 196
Namib Desert beetles 153
narwhals 126
nautiluses 15
neck 26, 192
neon flying squid 132
New Caledonian crows 176–7
nine-banded armadillos 196
nocturnal animals 21–3
noises 11–14, 16, 92, 98, 164, 182, 191
nose 11, 14, 15, 66, 113–15
nudibranchs 15

oarfish 127
octopuses 15, 40
odors 15, 26–7, 115–17, 175
oldest land animal 199
olms 66

Trademark notices

Frisbee is a trademark of Wham-O

Meet the FACTopians

Julie Beer is an author and editor based in California. Julie has written numerous books for National Geographic Kids on everything from national parks to space to her favorite subject of all—animals! When researching facts for this book, she knew she had to include one about sea otters. Her favorite fact is that sea otters store a special rock under their armpits in case they need to crack open food, such as clams. They're cute and clever!

Andy Smith is an award-winning illustrator. A graduate of the Royal College of Art, London, U.K., he creates artwork that has an optimistic, handmade feel. Creating the illustrations for *Animal FACTopia!* brought even more surprises, from lipstick-wearing fish to overheated chameleons! Andy's favorite fact to draw was Tillman the bulldog skateboarding in New York's Times Square. Andy also loved creating the blue tang fish, which looks a lot like his artist palette, but he's also very worried about the titan beetle snapping his pencils in half.

Lawrence Morton is an art director and designer based in London, U.K. Though he has worked on some of the world's leading fashion magazines, Lawrence has never had as much fun as when he was working on *Animal FACTopia!* As a left-hander, he was taken by the fact that male cats are more likely to be left-pawed. His favorite fact is that Isabela Island in the Galápagos is shaped like a seahorse!

Sources

Scientists and other experts are discovering new incredible animal facts and updating information all the time. This is why our FACTopia team has checked that every fact in this book is based on multiple trustworthy sources and their work has been verified by the Britannica team. Of the hundreds of sources used in this book, here is a list of key websites we consulted.

News Organizations
askabiologist.asu.edu
bbc.com
cbc.ca
cnn.com
kids.nationalgeographic.com
nationalgeographic.com
nationalgeographic.org
newscientist.com
npr.org
nytimes.com
pbs.org
sciencedaily.com
sciencemag.org
scientificamerican.com
smithsonianmag.com
slate.com
time.com
washingtonpost.com
wired.com

Government, Scientific, and Academic Organizations
academic.eb.com
allaboutbirds.org
animaldiversity.org
audubon.org
awf.org
batcon.org
britannica.com
fws.gov
galapagosconservation.org.uk
iucn.org
jstor.org
loc.gov
marinemammalcenter.org
merriam-webster.com
nature.com
ncbi.nlm.nih.gov

nps.gov
oceanconservancy.org
oceanservice.noaa.gov
penguinsinternational.org
pnas.org
royalsocietypublishing.org
sciencedirect.com
spaceplace.nasa.gov

Museums and Zoos
amnh.org
animals.sandiegozoo.org
floridamuseum.ufl.edu
kids.sandiegozoo.org
nationalzoo.si.edu
nhm.ac.uk
seaworld.org
si.edu

Other Websites
akc.org
atlasobscura.com
guinnessworldrecords.com
nwf.org
panthera.org
space.com
worldwildlife.org
wwf.org.uk

Picture Credits

The publisher would like to thank the following for permission to reproduce their photographs and illustrations. While every effort has been made to credit images, the publisher apologizes for any errors or omissions and will be pleased to make any necessary corrections in future editions of the book.

Cover Images: Penguin Alexey Seafarer/Shutterstock; Chameleon PetlinDmitry/Shutterstock

6 (ctr) Dirk Ercken/Shutterstock; 6 (lo) Lillian Tveit/Dreamstime; 8 Barbara Ash/Alamy; 11 SeDm/Shutterstock; 12 meunierd/Shutterstock; 17 Mike_shots/Shutterstock; 19 Annette Shaff/Shutterstock; 20 Oliver Thompson-Holmes/Alamy; 21 BIOSPHOTO/Alamy; 23 Abhishek Sah Photography/Shutterstock; 24-25 Lillian Tveit/Dreamstime; 27 Horst Bierau/Moment Open/Getty Images; 28-29 Marisa Estivill/Shutterstock; 30-31 Albert Beukhof/Shutterstock; 32-33 Mike Pellinni/Shutterstock; 35 BIOSPHOTO/Alamy; 36 Hany Rizk/EyeEm/Getty Images; 37 Elena Veselova/Dreamstime; 38-39 D. Parer and E. Parer-Cook/Minden Pictures; 41 PetlinDmitry/Shutterstock; 42 takmat71/Shutterstock; 43 Eric Isselee/Shutterstock; 44 Trent Townsend/Shutterstock; 45 Sarah2/Shutterstock; 46 Kuttelvaserova Stuchelova/Shutterstock; 47 Blazej Lyjak/Shutterstock; 50-51 Marko Steffensen/Alamy; 52-53 Sasha Samardzija/Shutterstock; 54-55 Slavianin/Shutterstock; 56-57 Martin Pelanek/Shutterstock; 57 (tail) Valentyna Chukhlyebova/Shutterstock; 58-59 (up) ipolsone/Shutterstock; 59 ctr Petr Ganaj/Shutterstock; 60 Aleksandar Dickov/Dreamstime; 61 Laura Romin/Alamy; 62-63 Pics516/Dreamstime; 64 BIOSPHOTO/Alamy; 67 Kirsten Wahlquist/Shutterstock; 69 Sibmens/Dreamstime; 70 Kerry Hill/Dreamstime; 72 3Dstock/Shutterstock; 73 Luna Vandoorne/Shutterstock; 74-75 Dave Watts/Alamy; 76 iacomino FRiMAGES/Shutterstock; 77 Nikolai Sorokin/Dreamstime; 78-79 (up) Fotoeye75/Dreamstime; 79 (le) effe45/Shutterstock; 79 (rt) Kazakovmaksim/Dreamstime; 80-81 Joe Sohm/Dreamstime; 83 (le) Andrey_Kuzmin/Shutterstock; 83 (rt) Sonsedska Yuliia/Shutterstock; 85 B. Saxton, (NRAO/AUI/NSF) from data provided by M. Goss, et al.; 86-87 (up) IP Galanternik D.U./iStockphoto/Getty Images; 87 Alexey Seafarer/Shutterstock; 88-89 Rich Carey/Shutterstock; 90 Volodymyr Burdiak/Shutterstock; 91 Nerssesyan/Shutterstock; 94 Sergey Uryadnikov/Shutterstock; 95 Jesse Nguyen/Shutterstock; 96 Eric Isselee/Shutterstock; 98 (up) monticello/Shutterstock; 98 (lo) evaurban/Shutterstock; 99 Cubanito/Dreamstime; 100-101 yevgeniy11/Shutterstock; 103 Antonella865/Dreamstime; 105 Dr Neil Overy/Science Photo Library RF/Getty Images; 106-107 Russ Heinl/Shutterstock; 108 Lightfieldstudiosprod/Dreamstime; 109 Somrerk Witthayanant/Shutterstock; 110 Realstock/Shutterstock; 111 (up) Deyangeorgiev/Dreamstime; 111 (lo) Volodymyr Byrdyak/Dreamstime; 112-113 Digital Storm/Shutterstock; 114-115 Astrid Gast/Shutterstock; 116 Erni/Shutterstock; 117 Vidas/Shutterstock; 119 Steve Adams/iStockphoto/Getty Images; 120 (ctr) TangoFoxtrot2018/Shutterstock; 120 (lo) Steven J. Kazlowski/Alamy; 121 Oktay Ortakcioglu/MediaProduction/E+/Getty Images; 123 Eric Isselee/Shutterstock; 125 Ken Backer/Dreamstime; 126 Dotted Yeti/Shutterstock; 128 Aleksandra Stepanova/Dreamstime; 129 Andersastphoto/Dreamstime; 130-131 Austin Paz/iStockphoto/Getty Images; 133 (up) Tamil Selvam/Shutterstock; 133 (lo) Shmelly50/Shutterstock; 134-135 Norbert Probst/imageBROKER RF/Getty Images; 136 (up) Martin Mecnarowski/Shutterstock; 136-137 JovanaMilanko/iStockphoto/Getty Images; 138 blickwinkel/Alamy; 139 Eric Isselee/Shutterstock; 140-141 buddeewiangngorn/123RF; 143 Steve Byland/Shutterstock; 144 back Damsea/Shutterstock; 144 (lo) Kisneborosmaria/Dreamstime; 145 (up le) Muellek Josef/Shutterstock; 145 (up back) Rich Carey/Shutterstock; 145 (lo) incamerastock/Alamy; 146 Artitwpd/Dreamstime; 147 Konrad Zelazowski/Alamy; 148 (door) Aliaksey Dobrolinski/Shutterstock; 148-149 New Africa/Shutterstock; 150 kai egan/Shutterstock; 151 davemhuntphotography/Shutterstock; 152 massdon/Shutterstock; 154 Jason Prince/iStockphoto/Getty Images; 155 nechaevkon/Shutterstock; 156 Brett Hondow/Shutterstock; 157 Larry N Young/iStockphoto/Getty Images; 158 karinabaumgart/123RF; 159 V_E/Shutterstock; 160-161 M_a_y_a/E+_Getty Images; 162 kojoty/123RF; 163 LouieLea/Shutterstock; 164 Coulanges/Shutterstock; 166-167 Iciar Cano Fondevila/Dreamstime; 168-169 scubaluna/iStockphoto/Getty Images; 170 Ondrej Prosicky/Shutterstock; 171 Debra Boast/Dreamstime; 172-173 cbimages/Alamy; 172-173 (back) Lubo Ivanko/Shutterstock; 175 Jacques Descloitres, MODIS LRRT/NASA/GSFC; 176 Daniel Prudek/Shutterstock; 177 Matt Knoth/Shutterstock; 178 (up) Martin Bech/Shutterstock; 178 (lo) Luciana Tancredo/Shutterstock; 180-181 Bruno Pacha/Shutterstock; 182-183 sabine_lj/Shutterstock; 184 Huseyin Faik/Alamy; 186 Laura Dts/Shutterstock; 188-189 Kurit afshen/Shutterstock; 190 Dirk Ercken/Shutterstock; 192 Dennis van de Water/Shutterstock; 195 Azahara Perez/Shutterstock; 197 surbs279/iStockphoto/Getty Images; 198 Morphart Creation/Shutterstock

BRITANNICA
BOOKS

Britannica Books is an imprint of What on Earth Publishing,
published in collaboration with Britannica, Inc.
Allington Castle, Maidstone, Kent ME16 0NB, United Kingdom
30 Ridge Road Unit B, Greenbelt, Maryland, 20770, United States

First published in the United States in 2023

Text copyright © 2023 What on Earth Publishing Ltd. and Britannica, Inc.
Illustrations copyright © 2023 Andy Smith
Trademark notices on page 204. Picture credits on page 207.

All rights reserved. No part of this publication may be reproduced or transmitted in any form or
by any means, electronic or mechanical, including photocopying, recording, or any information
storage or retrieval system, without permission in writing from the publishers. Requests for
permission to make copies of any part of this work should be directed to
info@whatonearthbooks.com.

Written by Julie Beer
Illustrated by Andy Smith
Designed by Lawrence Morton
Edited by WonderLab Group, LLC
Picture research by Annette Kiesow
Indexed by Connie Binder

Encyclopaedia Britannica
Alison Eldridge, Managing Editor; Michele Rita Metych, Fact Checking Supervisor

Britannica Books
Nancy Feresten, Publisher; Natalie Bellos, Editorial Director; Meg Osborne, Assistant Editor;
Andy Forshaw, Art Director; Alenka Oblak, Production Manager

Library of Congress Cataloging-in-Publication Data available upon request

ISBN: 9781913750732
Printed in India
1 3 5 7 9 10 8 6 4 2
whatonearthbooks.com
britannica-books.com

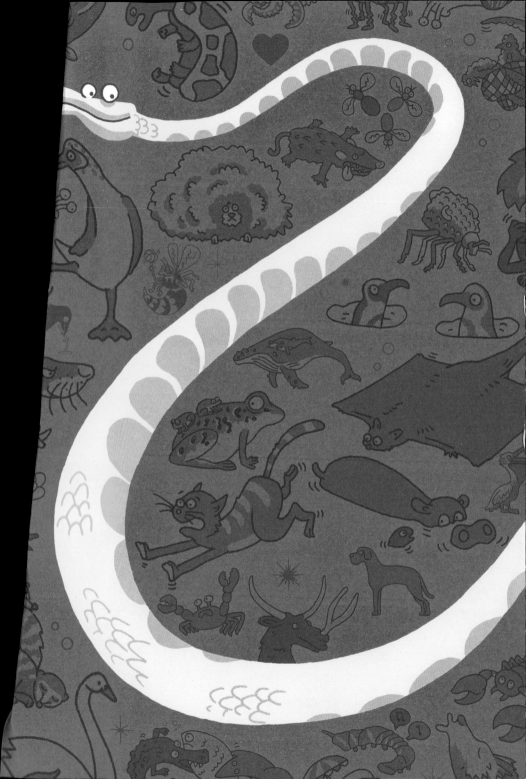

Think. Seek. Play. Le
Britannica.

Your family's key
to discovering
the amazingly weird
and strangely true.

Or visit
premium.britannica.com/learn